Six-Word Lessons on Winning with Today's Media

How do You get News Coverage?

Know the audience you're reaching for.

Define your audience. Do you want to reach the general public or a smaller segment like retired people, parents, business owners, an ethnic community, or young people? The audience you're trying to reach will determine which news outlets you should approach. It will also determine which individual reporters you should contact.

Six-Word Lessons on
WINNING WITH TODAY'S MEDIA

100 Lessons to Control Your Message & Avoid Media Blunders

Mary Waldmann

Published by Pacelli Publishing
Bellevue, Washington

Six-Word Lessons on Winning with Today's Media - 6wordlessons.com

All rights reserved. No part of this book may be reproduced or transmitted in any form or by any means, electronic or mechanical including photocopying, recording or by any information storage or retrieval system, without the written permission of the publisher, except where permitted by law.

Limit of Liability: While the author and the publisher have used their best efforts in preparing this book, they make no representation or warranties with respect to accuracy or completeness of the content of this book. The advice and strategies contained herein may not be suitable for your situation. Consult with a professional when appropriate

Copyright © 2014, 2017 by Mary Waldmann

Published by Pacelli Publishing
9905 Lake Washington Blvd. NE, #D-103
Bellevue, Washington 98004
Pacellipublishing.com

ISBN-10: 1-933750-41-3
ISBN-13: 978-1-933750-41-5

Author photo by Yuen Lui Photography
Cover photo by microgen@123RF.com
Cover and interior design by Pacelli Publishing

Introduction

When and why should you talk to news reporters? If you have a business, project, or community cause to promote, speaking with the news media can be the most efficient and cost-effective way to reach an audience. If you're running for local office or taking a stand on community issues, it's vital to have a good working relationship with the news media.

If your company or organization is dealing with a public problem or negative news story, reporters may be contacting you. If you're dealing with damage control, you've got to get your side of the story out. Don't wait until a crisis arises to learn the basic skills of dealing with news media representatives.

Being a prepared and effective media spokesperson can be a tremendous personal and professional asset. Many businesses, projects and causes fail for lack of public recognition and support. Don't let yours be one of them. Your competence in talking to the news media can be an asset to your company or organization. You can be the one to whom they turn.

Good media relations don't happen accidentally. You have to put some effort into it. But you don't need expensive media training. These six-word lessons will teach you everything you need to know in order to deal with the news media, from the ground rules to insider tips and techniques. While technology, social media and the speed of deadlines have changed, the rules remain the same. Follow them and you can make your encounters with the news media positive, and even enjoyable.

Acknowledgements

Many thanks to my wonderful husband, Ray Waldmann, for his support and excellent editing. Thanks, too, to Jackie Livingston, Jerry Hendin and Del Hoffman who reviewed the early draft and provided helpful suggestions.

Table of Contents

How do You get News Coverage?..7

When a Reporter Calls You First..19

How to Prepare for an Interview..31

When it's Your Turn to Speak..43

You CAN Deal with Difficult Questions..55

Handle Radio Interviews Like a Pro..67

Tips for a Stellar Television Interview..79

How to Call a News Conference..91

The Art of Post-Interview Follow-up..103

The "Ten Commandments" for Media Interviews........................115

Six-Word Lessons on Winning with Today's Media

What message will you give them?

If you can't summarize your story in three sentences or less, you don't have a story. What message do you want to leave with the readers or viewers? What would you want as your headline? Write it down, then edit to make your key message as concise and direct as possible.

Search for the likely media outlets.

Most libraries have media directories to which you can refer or you can use online search engines. Be sure to look for specialty publications which reach your target audience. Target the ones most likely to be interested in your subject. (You can also use social media, but that's another book.)

Do some research on each outlet.

What are the demographics of the outlet's audience? If it's a publication, how often is it published? Do they publish op-ed articles? If it's a television or radio station, do they want straight news, or do they air talk shows? If it's a talk show, who is the host and what time of day does it air? Are community billboard or community service spots an option?

Find out who covers the topic.

In larger news media organizations, reporters are assigned to particular beats. For instance, reporters may have individual business, environmental, community, consumer affairs and political reporters. Smaller stations and publications may have only a few reporters covering it all. Call to find out who covers your topic.

Do some homework on the reporter.

Read some articles written by the print reporter. Listen to the station. If you plan to approach a talk show, by all means listen to it a time or two to learn the format, tone and style of the host. Try Google, Facebook or a similar source to learn a little about the reporter's background. Does he have a particular point of view?

Prepare an interesting and positive story.

Expand on your three-sentence-or-less message. Explain a little of the background on your story. Use colorful words and examples. Think in terms of the news "hook." Why should the reporter want to cover your story? Your message is a product and you have to sell it to the reporter if you want to get coverage.

Be sure to marshal your facts.

Always make sure your facts are correct. Mistakes can be damaging, both with the story outcome and to your credibility. When you can, cite statistics, studies or outside experts who support your position. These will all increase your credibility, but make sure they're accurate. You want to be viewed as a reliable source in the future.

Don't be afraid to call reporters.

Most reporters now prefer to receive news releases electronically. Check their websites for details on how to e-mail your material. You can follow up with a telephone call a few days later. Don't tell them they "should" cover your story, but suggest why they might find your information newsworthy.

Put together a complete press kit.

If you're sending more than just a news release, such as a fact sheet, photo or bio, remember to put your company or organization name, your name, telephone number(s) and e-mail address on each item. You may want to add a "press kit" section to your website if you have one.

Six-Word Lessons on Winning with Today's Media

When a Reporter Calls You First

Start by taking a deep breath.

Don't agree to an interview or jump into a response without first taking a deep breath and quickly gathering your thoughts. Who is calling and who do they represent? Is this an issue you should be addressing in the media? Are they looking for a future interview, or do they want an immediate telephone interview?

Find out why they called YOU.

Are you a recognized figure with this company, issue or story? If not, politely ask why they called you specifically. Did they see a previous story that quoted or cited you? Have they heard you speak? Read something you've written? Did someone else suggest they speak to you? Have you been visible on this or similar issues in the past?

Ask questions about the interview format.

Do they want a telephone interview now or at a future time? Do they want to come to your office or other site related to the story? Will the interview be live or taped? If it's a talk show program, will there be guests besides you? If so, who will they be? Approximately how long will the interview run?

What is the likely story angle?

You can ask, politely, if the reporter already has a story angle in mind. Is it about a controversy? Investigative piece? Human interest story? Profile piece? Knowing the story angle will help you tailor your message, but don't be surprised if they only say, "It's just developing" or "We'll see."

Is the story positive or negative?

A reporter is not likely to tell you this, but you may already know or be able to sense if the story is likely to be a good one or bad one for you. If you think it's negative, be prepared for difficult questions and try to buy some time to respond. But don't assume that it's negative. It may not be, or you may be able to influence the outcome.

16

Deadlines are crucial to a story.

Every media outlet operates on a different set of deadlines. These days, news cycles are very short and around the clock. Always ask what the reporter's deadline is. If you need to get back to them with answers or information, you MUST do it before the deadline. Failure to do so means you won't be covered or, worse, they might say you had no comment or print half-facts.

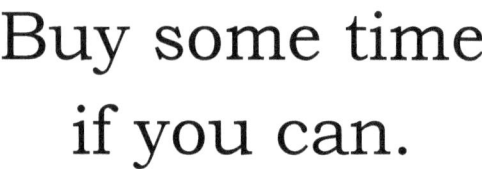

Buy some time if you can.

If the interview is immediate, try to place the reporter on hold for a minute while you clear your office or find a quiet conference room where you can shut the door. Make sure you turn your phone off or have calls held. If the reporter isn't on immediate deadline and you need more information, ask if you can call back within a reasonable amount of time.

Ask who else they're talking to.

You can ask, but always politely, who else the reporter is talking to. Are they people who support your position, opponents or competitors? Reporters like controversy and always try to get "the other side." This will give you a better sense of the story's angle and how it may develop. But know that they may not tell you.

Suggest additional people they might call.

You can suggest other people the reporter might contact who can give additional information or help buttress your position. Be sure to say why the other person(s) could be helpful to their story. Like anyone else, reporters appreciate anyone who can help make their jobs easier. If there are other people in your organization who can amplify on your story, offer to arrange it.

You have the right to decline.

You always have the right to decline an interview. If you're not the appropriate person, tell the reporter who they should call or offer to have that person call back. If you definitely don't want to answer questions, try to give a reason, such as "I don't have that information," or "It's an internal (or personnel) matter," or "We're still looking at the issue."

How to Prepare for an Interview

Anticipate questions you might be asked.

If you've asked the right questions and know your subject, you should be able to predict some of the questions. If you have time, even if it's only a few minutes before a call-back, make a list of the questions you expect to be asked, then develop answers that are positive and concise. Get more information if you need it.

Prepare a positive and concise message.

Keep it concise—think in terms of headline quotes or thirty-second sound bites. If you approached the reporter, you should already have done this. If the reporter's call was unexpected and the interview is immediate, take a minute at least to gather your thoughts. If you're given the time, write down the essence of your story.

Be ready to develop your story.

If you have prepared for the call, or if you are given time to prepare, review the reasons your story is important, timely and relevant to the reporter and their audience. Use examples or anecdotal information. Cite your own experiences. Plan how to segue from each of the anticipated questions back to your positive message.

Time permitting, ask others for advice.

It always helps to get additional input and suggestions. If you have time, ask others in your organization, company or campaign what questions they think might be asked. They may be able to provide answers to questions or additional information you can use for the interview. Find out if others have already spoken to reporters on this subject.

If you have time, get practice.

As time allows, practice by having someone ask you the questions, especially if you anticipate negative ones. This gives you an opportunity to refine your answers and increases the odds that you'll remember what you wanted to say. Major political candidates always do this, especially before televised debates. Take a lesson from them.

Visualization is an effective preparation tool.

When you close your eyes and visualize yourself doing something, the same brain neurons fire as if you were actually doing the activity. Positive visualization can improve your performance and make it more likely you'll remember your desired story and responses.

Don't be afraid to get personal.

You want to come across as a real person. In telling your story, don't be afraid to use examples from your own experience or cite your background as an expert on your subject. Be genuine. Being a little personal will increase your likeability and we tend to see people we like as being more credible.

Beforehand, avoid alcohol, coffee or tea.

Alcohol will not relax you, in fact it dulls the edge you need to carry on a good interview. Too much coffee gives you the jitters, which you're likely to feel as stage fright. Even in small amounts, alcohol, coffee and tea have an astringent effect on your mouth tissue. A dry mouth is a handicap and a distraction that you don't want to experience.

Don't be spooked by "stage fright."

Whether it's comfortable or adversarial, doing an interview is a stressful experience. This is likely to cause an adrenaline surge, with elevated heartbeat and respiration rates. When it happens, don't panic or tell yourself you have stage fright. Instead, say to yourself, "I'm energized—I have that edge I need to do my best job." Then take a deep breath and exhale.

Just "on time" is too late.

If the interview has been scheduled for a specific time, try to be ready at least 20 minutes early. If the reporter arrives early, you'll be ready. If you're traveling to the interview, allow ample time for traffic, parking or delays. If it's a television interview, you'll want time to meet the camera crew. You'll be more relaxed and confident if you're not feeling rushed.

Six-Word Lessons on Winning with Today's Media

When it's Your Turn to Speak

Remember that you are the expert.

The reporter is talking to you because she thinks you have an answer, valuable information or important insight. If you weren't an expert on your subject or issue, she probably wouldn't be calling you. Keep this in mind and it should help you feel more confident and relaxed. Use positive self-talk: "I know what I'm talking about."

Slow down and take your time.

Some people have a tendency to speak faster when they are nervous, so slow your pace a little. Similarly, many of us tend to anticipate the next thing we want to say while the reporter is still asking the question. There's nothing wrong with a thoughtful pause. Use it to slow the conversation and to think about what you really want to say before you start to speak.

Always strive to use complete sentences.

Don't start a response with "Because…" or similar words. Always begin with a subject word. This will make it easier to quote you. Avoid "uh's, "so's and similar placeholder words, which make it simple for reporters to cut and splice your comments in audio or video recordings. This allows them to more easily quote you out of context.

Don't give "yes" or "no" answers.

Don't make the interview a tennis match where your objective is just to get the ball back to the interviewer. View it as a football game where you take the ball and run with it. Instead of saying "yes" or "no," speak a complete sentence and then amplify it with examples or additional information, or segue back to your primary message.

Please be careful when using humor.

A humorous remark can easily be misunderstood. Your message is important and you don't want to appear frivolous or dismissive. On talk shows, a little natural humor can make you appear more relaxed and personable, but beware of anything that can be misunderstood or misconstrued.

Don't say anything ironic or sarcastic.

Irony and sarcasm depend mostly upon the tone of your voice, so can easily be misinterpreted in print. In radio and television interviews as well, listeners may miss the irony. You want to appear professional and positive, not sarcastic or disrespectful. It's best to avoid irony and sarcasm altogether.

Don't correct your very minor misstatements.

Always correct your misstatement of fact or one that affects your message. But in television and radio interviews, don't correct little things like a garbled word. Backing up to correct it only draws a big red box around your error when the odds are the listener wouldn't have noticed it in the first place.

Keep your tone easy and conversational.

This is particularly important in radio and television interviews. Always be polite. Use the reporter's name occasionally. Don't interrupt except when a hostile radio or television reporter is making a speech rather than asking a question. Don't raise your voice if you disagree with the premise of a question.

If nervous, pitch your voice lower.

In many people, nervousness can cause the voice to rise in pitch. This will make you sound shrill or angry. When you're doing a radio or television interview and you find yourself doing this, slow down and consciously pitch your voice a little lower and slower.

Try this cure for dry mouth.

An excessively dry mouth can be the result of adrenaline. It's a distraction and can affect your speech. If you find yourself experiencing a dry mouth, gently bite down a few times on the tip of your tongue to get saliva flowing again. A mint just prior to the interview may help prevent the problem in the future.

Six-Word Lessons on Winning with Today's Media

You CAN Deal with Difficult Questions

Role-play your Q-&-A in advance.

If you're preparing for a difficult interview, ALWAYS role-play the questions and answers in advance. Then when you hear the question, you won't have to struggle for a response. The repetition of actually saying the answers as you've perfected them increases the likelihood that those words will come to mind under pressure.

Listen with care to each question.

Listen to the question all the way through before you start thinking about your answer. If you're anticipating your answer, you may not fully understand the question or may miss a key element. Also listen for nuance. The reporter's tone of voice may give you additional insight.

Make sure you understand the question.

If you're not quite sure what the reporter is asking, request clarification. If you try to answer a question you don't fully understand, you're likely to get yourself into trouble. Don't formulate your response until you're absolutely sure exactly what is being asked of you.

If you don't know, say so.

Don't ever bluff. If you don't know the answer to a question, be honest and say so. Then offer to get back to the reporter later with the answer or suggest someone else in your company or organization they might call. Better yet, offer to ask that person to call the reporter.

Always admit when you were wrong.

If you, your organization or business has been caught in a mistake or clear wrong-doing, never deny it. You'll only make the reporter press harder to prove the allegation and you'll prolong the story cycle. Admit the problem and then say, in positive terms, what you are doing to rectify the situation.

Never catch a "ball of worms."

This is a question that actually contains two or more separate questions. Don't try to untangle them yourself. You'll be distracted from the first answer by trying to remember the second or third part of the question. Say "There seems to be more than one question there. Which one would you like me to address first?"

Don't accept a negative as true.

This is the, "When did you stop beating your wife?" question. "Don't say, "We never..." or "It's not true that..." and then repeat the negative. Always respond with a positive statement that refutes or negates the assumption. Don't appear defensive. Then go back to the story you want to tell.

Avoid guessing when asked hypothetical questions.

Don't speculate about future events or actions by other people. Stick with what you know to be true. Say "I can't predict the future, but what I do know is ..." and go back to your central message. However, if you have accurate data to back you up, you can say, "If this, then that." But be careful.

Never let a reporter bait you.

Reporters know that if they can get you riled up, you're more likely to depart from your message or say something you'll wish you hadn't said. Some reporters will deliberately bait you about a controversial subject to get more quotable remarks. Don't take the bait by getting angry or flustered. Stick with your message.

50

Don't get trapped by repetitive questions.

If you've said that you can't or won't answer a specific question, don't be surprised if it's asked again. Reporters know that if they keep asking the same question, they may wear you down and you'll eventually respond. Don't let yourself get frustrated. Simply respond by reiterating your polite refusal.

Six-Word Lessons on Winning with Today's Media

Handle Radio Interviews Like a Pro

Know how long you can speak.

If you'll have ten minutes on a radio show, you can really expand on your story. If you have only three minutes, you have to concentrate on the basic message. You may launch into a good presentation, only to be cut off before you get to the guts of it. Always start with the most important part of your message.

52

Go ahead and use simple notes.

In a radio interview, you won't be seen by the audience, so you can prepare in advance by bringing a simple outline of your key message. Include the major things you want to say about it. Jot down statistics or other information you'll want to cite. But keep it to one page and use bullet points for easy reference.

Try to eliminate any potential distractions.

If you're doing the interview from your home or place of work, remove distractions in advance. Make sure you have a quiet place and that you are free from interruptions. Don't have other people in the room. If there are others, don't let them speak. Don't look out a window. Clear the desk of everything but your interview notes.

54

Get as comfortable as you can.

Wear comfortable clothing that doesn't restrict your breathing. If you're in the office or at home, sit in a comfortable chair. If you're in a radio studio, make sure the microphone is at the right height so you don't have to lean or stretch. But don't get too relaxed. Sit up and stay alert.

You must speak with vocal dynamics.

In radio, you can't use facial expression or hand gestures to communicate so it's essential that you use really good vocal dynamics. Use emphasis. Let your voice show authority, conviction, concern, or enthusiasm for your subject. Avoid monotones or ending your sentences with a rising inflection. Smile—the audience can hear it in your voice.

"Plant" calls for a call-in program.

If you're doing a call-in radio program, always ask at least one or more friend or colleague to call in with a question that you want to answer. You can't count on strangers. Also, the more positive questions are called in, the less likely that negative callers will get through.

Suggest questions you want to answer.

You can give the interviewer a few questions that you'd like to be asked by saying, "Here are some things I think your audience would find of interest" or, "Here are some questions I'm frequently asked." You can provide a short written list in advance, or bring it to the interview.

58

Remember that it's a live conversation.

You're not making a speech, you're conducting a conversation. Be responsive to the questions. Keep your tone conversational. Use the reporter's name. Don't make your answers too long—be concise. Be authoritative, but don't talk down to the reporter or the audience.

Use words that paint a picture.

Help the audience to "see" what you're saying. Use vivid or colorful words to tell your story. Use personal anecdotes to illustrate your message. Describe what may result if the problem you're talking about isn't addressed or if a program is successful. Ask them to visualize the consequences.

Old-fashioned advice: Sit up straight.

Frequently you'll be seated in a nice cushy chair. Resist the temptation to relax back into it. You'll have a clearer, more dynamic voice if you breathe from your diaphragm, which requires that you sit up straight with good posture. You'll also sound more alert and professional.

Six-Word Lessons on Winning with Today's Media

Tips for a Stellar Television Interview

Know if it's live or taped.

If the program is live, you'll be seen and heard directly "as is." If it's taped, your comments may be edited, so be particularly careful not to use "uh's. If it's a talk show taped for later broadcast, treat it as a live broadcast. If it's a program, they may use excerpts or quotes in the news if you say something controversial.

Find out when the interview airs.

Not only do you want to see it, but you want to know who else will be viewing your interview. Time of day determines this. An early weekend show will have fewer viewers than one that airs on the news or in prime time. Afternoon talk show audiences differ in demographics from those of morning news programs.

Wear clothing that works on camera.

Your clothing should be appropriate to your position, your likely audience and your subject. When in doubt, dress more conservatively. Avoid large prints, flashy ties, or excessive jewelry which can be visual distractions. Red attracts attention so a red tie or deep lipstick is appropriate. Women, make sure your clothing covers your knees when you're seated.

Arrive early; size up the setting.

You'll want to know what's in the background. Is the interview in a studio or outdoors? If the reporter is coming to you, be ready to suggest a simple setting or one appropriate to the subject. Make sure you know where the camera is located. If there are more than one, find out where the red lights are located that indicate which one is in use.

Make friends with the camera crew.

Introduce yourself to the camera crew. A friendly camera man can give you some advantages on camera angles. Chatting a bit with the crew can help you relax. But always remember that they have a job to do, so don't get in the way or get overly conversational.

Dynamic facial expressions make a difference.

The look on your face can add to or detract from the impact of your presentation. If you're enthusiastic, concerned or angry about an issue, let it show in your facial expression. Speak with your eyes as well as your mouth. Don't be deadpan. Practice by talking into a mirror.

Interviewer? Camera? Where you should look.

As a general rule, you should always look at the interviewer. You want the conversation to look natural. However, if you are taping an advertisement, public service announcement or something similar, you'll want to look directly into the camera. Imagine a smiling face on the lens and talk to that.

Body language is a crucial concern.

Your body language can show confidence or be a giveaway to nervousness. Avoid fidgeting with your hands or tapping your foot. Use hand gestures to emphasize and illustrate your points, but don't keep repeating the same few gestures. We have a tendency to nod indicating our understanding, but don't nod in assent when a question is being asked.

A smile goes a long way.

When you're smiling, you appear more friendly and positive. Smiling also helps to relax you. However, avoid smiling when the subject is serious or you're being asked a negative question. Inappropriate smiling is an interview killer. But by all means, smile when you're enthused about your subject.

Always assume the camera is on.

From the minute the camera is set up or you arrive in the studio, assume that everything you say and do may be recorded. If you're chatting informally with the reporter prior to the official interview, be aware that the camera may actually be on and act accordingly. Don't relax until you've left the studio or the reporter has departed or hung up.

Six-Word Lessons on Winning with Today's Media

Six-Word Lessons on Winning with Today's Media

How to Call a News Conference

Limit news conferences to major announcements.

Be realistic about the importance of what you have to say. You don't want to hold a news conference and have no one show up. However, if it's a major story and you want to communicate your message to a large number of media representatives, then a news conference is the way to go.

Put together a relevant media list.

Consult a media directory or online resource to compile the news outlets in your area. Don't overlook the smaller ones, including specialty publications, which may have more time or space to cover your story. Make sure you know which person on staff to alert. You may want to send an advisory to both the reporter and the overall editor or news director.

Choose the time for maximum coverage.

Television requires time to edit footage, so hold your news conference in the morning. You'll get much better coverage of a conference early in the week rather than on a Friday afternoon. Avoid the weekend. Make sure the location is easily accessible and has adequate parking. Set up a podium and chairs for reporters, and leave room for camera crews.

Send a media advisory in advance.

Send a media advisory in advance, stating the subject, the speaker(s), the date and time, as well as the location of the news conference. Include your name, organization and contact information. You may want to include a news release embargoed until the time of the conference. That way your story can be reported even when a reporter can't physically attend.

Be prepared with a printed statement.

Be prepared with copies of the statement or announcement to be made. Date it for immediate release. Make the statement short—maximum one page only. Stick to the guts of your story—the key points. It should be concise and well-written. This will serve as the script for your principal's opening statement. Make sure to have sufficient copies.

Provide additional handouts when they're useful.

If your statement is heavy on statistics or data, or if you are using charts, provide them on printed pages separate from the statement. Keep them simple, with only as much detail as needed. Use bullet points. Pass these out to reporters as they arrive. Be sure to include contact information.

Always start at the appointed time.

A reporter's time is valuable. They have invested their time in your news conference, so don't waste it by running late. You won't make friends that way. Always begin exactly on time. If more than one principal will be available for questions, have them stand to the side and slightly behind the person making the statement.

Have someone else introduce the speaker.

Have someone other than the principal speaker announce that it's time to begin. They should say that the principal will make a brief statement and then answer questions. They should also say how much time will be given for questions, and then introduce him or her.

Read your statement, then answer questions.

Your statement should have been practiced so you can deliver it smoothly. Deliver the opening and closing lines without looking down. Refer to the printed page when necessary, but make sure you maintain good eye contact with the entire room. Conclude with your key message, then say "And now I'll take your questions."

Limit the questions to your subject.

You have a message to convey. Don't let reporters ask questions that lead you away from your subject. Politely remind them that you are addressing this subject and that you will limit your comments today to that. If you want to answer an off-topic question, do so, then quickly segue back to your main message.

The Art of Post-Interview Follow-up

If you initiated it, say "Thanks."

If you requested the interview, send a short note of appreciation to the reporter thanking them for their time and interest. E-mails are fine, but handwritten notes make more of an impact. Taking time to say thank-you makes you more memorable so it's more likely they'll contact you in the future.

If you erred, always correct it.

If you later realize that you made a significant misstatement in your interview, or cited incorrect facts, immediately contact the reporter with the correct information. If you hang him out to dry with an inaccurate story, you'll make an enemy and certainly destroy your future credibility.

Additional information can always be sent.

If you were unable to answer a question at the time but promised to follow up with the information, do it in a timely fashion. If you subsequently think of additional information that might be useful to the reporter, go ahead and send it with a short cover note.

84

Good story? Tell the reporter that.

If you thought the story was particularly insightful, or well-written, send the reporter a note complimenting them on it. Give a specific reason you thought it was good. Everyone likes to receive positive feedback and reporters are no exception. However, avoid obvious flattery or insincerity.

Bad story? Don't be a complainer.

If you don't like the story but it is accurate, do not contact the reporter to complain about it. It's unprofessional. Figure out where you went wrong and resolve to do better next time. Similarly, don't complain if the story doesn't appear or if you're not mentioned. News priorities change.

Incorrect story? You can make corrections.

If the story is inaccurate, contact the reporter but don't say, "You were wrong." Instead, lay the blame on yourself. Say "Perhaps I wasn't clear enough in my explanation. What I meant to convey was…" You're objective is to get the right story out, not to prove who was right or wrong.

Try to maintain the reporter/source relationship.

If you'd like the reporter to continue using you as a resource, try to maintain a relationship by occasionally sending her further information about your cause or issue that you think she might find of interest. However, make sure it's pertinent to her beat and is something new.

88

But don't ever be a nuisance.

Know that reporters are inundated by calls, e-mails and news releases. You want to be viewed as a good resource, not a pest. Don't become a nuisance by sending them material that they aren't likely to want, and don't send things too frequently. Keep them happy to hear from you.

Ask for honest feedback from others.

Ask colleagues and friends to review the story that results from your interview and get their reactions. Was the message clear and persuasive? Did you look and sound convincing? Were there things that distracted them from your message? What are their suggestions for improvement?

90

Take time to learn from experience.

Were you prepared for the questions? Were there any surprises? Are there questions that you should have answered differently? Examine what went well and what didn't. How would you do it differently next time? Learn from the experience, but don't beat yourself up over mistakes.

Six-Word Lessons on Winning with Today's Media

The "Ten Commandments" for Media Interviews

Always have a clear, concise message.

Don't go into an interview without having a clear, concise message. If you are given extra time, you can expand on your message, but always start with a central theme that you can express in three sentences or less.

Keep going back to your message.

Don't give your message just one time. Use questions as an opportunity to segue back to your central theme. Repetition hammers the story home. Answer the question, then use it as a springboard to what YOU want to say. Stick with your message.

Do not ever, ever, EVER lie!

If you lie, the odds are great that you'll eventually be caught in the lie, destroying your credibility and fostering negative news coverage. The same is true for misleading information. You don't have to tell everything you know but don't lie or tell misleading half-truths.

Don't ever go "off the record."

Even though reporters may tell you that you are "off the record" or "just on background," there is a good chance they won't honor those promises. So if you don't want to see something in print or on the air, don't say it. Period.

Avoid using the response, "No comment."

If you're not going to answer the question, don't give a curt "No comment." If you can, give a brief explanation of why you won't comment. Otherwise, say, "I'm not going to respond to that question but what I can say is..." and go back to your message.

Don't exceed your authority or expertise.

Avoid getting lured out of your territory. If you don't have sufficient information, be honest and say so. If what's being asked goes beyond your authority in your company or organization, suggest they talk to someone else. Stick with YOUR message.

Always assume that you are "live."

Stay on message from the time the reporter enters the room or you enter the studio. Avoid cracking jokes before or after the interview—the microphone may still be on. Even if a print reporter isn't taking notes at the time, anything you say may be reported.

Never ask for an advance look.

Don't request an advance look at the article, story or film clip. You won't get it and you will look like an amateur. Similarly, never ask to approve quotes. It won't happen. Be prepared, do your best job, stick with your message and wait for the results.

Use all tools at your disposal.

Remember that you are your best visual aid. Use facial expressions and appropriate hand gestures to reinforce your message. When appropriate, let the backdrop for your interview reflect the story, such as an outdoor setting for an environmental story.

100

Don't ever fight with a reporter.

The old saying goes, "Never get into a fight with someone who buys ink by the barrel." It's excellent advice. Remember, the news organization always controls the story. If you get into a fight with the reporter or the editor, you are guaranteed to lose.

About the *Six-Word Lessons Series*

Legend has it that Ernest Hemingway was challenged to write a story using only six words. He responded with the story, "For sale: baby shoes, never worn." The story tickles the imagination. Why were the shoes never worn? The answers are left up to the reader's imagination.

This style of writing has a number of aliases: postcard fiction, flash fiction, and micro fiction. Lonnie Pacelli was introduced to this concept in 2009 by a friend, and started thinking about how this extreme brevity could apply to today's communication culture of text messages, tweets and Facebook posts. He wrote the first book, *Six-Word Lessons for Project Managers*, then started helping other authors write and publish their own books in the series.

The books all have six-word chapters with six-word lesson titles, each followed by a one-page description. They can be written by entrepreneurs who want to promote their businesses, or anyone with a message to share.

See the entire *Six-Word Lessons Series* at 6wordlessons.com

www.ingramcontent.com/pod-product-compliance
Lightning Source LLC
Chambersburg PA
CBHW070643050426
42451CB00008B/286